Dreamtoons

Dreamtoons

Jesse Reklaw

SHAMBHALA
Boston & London
2000

Dedicated to Hans Arp

SHAMBHALA PUBLICATIONS, INC.
HORTICULTURAL HALL
300 MASSACHUSETTS AVENUE
BOSTON, MASSACHUSETTS 02115
www.shambhala.com

Some of the strips in *Dreamtoons* originally appeared in
The Connection, Drawl, Dreamtime, Eugene Comic News, Factsheet 5,
The Fairfield/Westchester County Weekly, Funny Times, Generation Next,
Hartford Advocate, New Haven Advocate, Ottawa X-Press, Philadelphia Weekly,
The Pointer, Proper Gander, Quirks, The Rocket, San Diego Reader,
Seattle Weekly, Southwest File, Stuff, Valley Advocate,
VMAG, and *Weekly Alibi.*

9 8 7 6 5 4 3 2 1

First Edition

Printed in the United States of America

♾ This edition is printed on acid-free paper that meets the American
National Standards Institute Z39.48 Standard.

Distributed in the United States by Random House, Inc.,
and in Canada by Random House of Canada Ltd

LIBRARY OF CONGRESS CATALOGING-IN-PUBLICATION DATA
Reklaw, Jesse, 1971–
[Slow wave Selections]
Dreamtoons/Jesse Reklaw.—1st. ed.
p. cm.
ISBN 1-57062-573-5 (pbk.: alk. paper)
I. Title.
P{N6728.S56 R45 2000
741.5'973—dc21   99-087278

It Came from Below

Are you wasting one-third of your life at the pillow? Imagine the opportunities that a life without sleep would provide—you could work longer hours, have time to floss twice a day, and perhaps catch an extra sitcom or two. But seriously, the need for sleep is a frustrating reminder of human physicality, proof that we have earthly limits. Luckily there's an escape: between the ports of good night and good morning, the mind produces entertainment, like a feature film on a transatlantic submarine ride, except of course that this show is produced especially for you.

But the supremely personal nature of dreams is also a drawback: how can these amazing experiences be shared? Unlike the high points of last night's hit show, even the best dreams often leave friends and family bewildered. People actually get bored hearing about public nakedness and flying! With only clumsy words and gestures to convey this immensely subjective experience, dreams have gotten a bad reputation for putting their audiences to sleep.

In this book I hope to recharge dreams with their trademark oddity, thrills, and humor. For the past five years I have been translating the inner adventures of different people into a comic strip called *Slow Wave*, which has been printed by weekly papers in Seattle, Hartford, San Diego, Ottawa, Long Island, Philadelphia, Berkeley, and other cities. Dreams are submitted by readers of the strip in these papers, as well as online. From thousands of submissions, I have selected my favorite dreams—whether for their sheer silliness or for the intriguing tales they tell—then condensed them into four-panel strips. Where possible, I have also attempted to draw the likeness of each dreamer, based on a photograph or physical description.

So please come meet these folks and share their impossible encounters. Maybe you will discover dreams just like your own, or perhaps some you wish you'd had.

Acknowledgments

I would like to acknowledge my editors, Kendra Crossen Burroughs and Eden Steinberg, who made this book possible; Raven Hanna for constant help, suggestions, and modeling; the dreamers with their outrageously creative inventions; the editors who chose the *Slow Wave* comic strip for their newspapers: Jill MacDowell, Stewart Williams, Eric Scigliano, Jim Creskey, Murphy, Karen Unger, Joshua Mamis, Dan Caccavaro, Janet Reynolds, Lorraine Gengo, Christopher Johnson, John Mancini, Susan Wolpert, Raymond Lesser, Jim Holman, Paul Houston, Allison Clark, Chris Becker, A. Owsley, Thom Coby, Cathy Grubman, Don Kahle, Grady Roper; and all the online friends who supported this project with comments, dream submissions, correspondence, and also for spreading the word: Ranjit Bhatnagar, Lex Spahr, Uncle Aussie, Scott Bartell, James Livingston, Cinderella Walker, Skooch Sheehan, Mike Wooldridge, Brandon MacInnis, Amber Carvan, Andy Hartzell, Chris Aynesworth, Jason Harris, Zach Archer, Richard Wilkerson, and many more—thank you all!!!

Dreamtoons

"Dreaming permits each and every one of us to be quietly and safely insane every night of our lives."

DR. WILLIAM C. DEMENT

Stanford sleep researcher

I WAS LIVING IN AN APARTMENT BUILDING.

SUDDENLY IT TURNED INTO A GIANT CHICKEN AND WALKED AWAY WITH EVERYONE INSIDE.

bok bok!

IT STILL HAD WINDOWS AND STUFF, BUT IT WAS DEFINITELY A CHICKEN.

From a dream by Dale Novak

Giant Contact Lenses

I DREAMT I ORDERED NEW CONTACT LENSES, BUT THEY WERE THE SIZE OF PAPER PLATES.

THEN I SAW THAT THE INSTRUCTIONS INCLUDED ORIGAMI DIAGRAMS.

I TRIED TO FOLD MY LENSES INTO FROG AND CRANE SHAPES.

they're just too slippery!

FINALLY I GAVE UP AND TAPED ONE TO MY HEAD LIKE A VISOR.

i guess it helps.

From a dream by Emily Bick

ME AND FOUR OF MY FRIENDS WERE IN A FIELD. I HAD THIS CONTAINER OF CHOCOLATE MILK.

I DRANK IT AND STARTED LAUGHING, SPITTING MILK ALL OVER THEIR FACES.

SNORT!

NO ONE HAD ANY TOWELS.

use my **socks** to wipe your faces.

SO THEY DID. THEN WE LOOKED AND THEIR FACES HAD RUBBED OFF ON MY SOCKS!

this is my dream. i really had it.

From a dream by Alex J. Peck

WHEN WE ARE BORN, GOD GIVES EACH OF US A PAPER BAG. I FOUND MYSELF (AND MY BAG) IN HIS PRESENCE.

THE LIGHT WAS BLINDING! I PUT THE BAG OVER MY HEAD AND TORE EYE-HOLES SO I COULD SEE A LITTLE BIT.

AS I BECAME MORE ENLIGHTENED, I TORE LARGER HOLES.

EVENTUALLY THERE WAS MORE HOLE THAN BAG.

I FELT I HAD GRADUATED FROM THE "PAPER BAG" STAGE, SO GOD GAVE ME A PAIR OF SUNGLASSES.

purple! my favorite!

From a dream by Pete Petersen

PEOPLE COME TO INTERVIEW MY PET RABBIT WITHOUT MY PERMISSION. THEY BRUSH BY ME AND SHOVE THEIR MICRO- PHONES IN HER FACE.

how has your life been?

yeah—in that **cage**.

IN HORROR, I FRANTICALLY SEARCH MY MIND TO SEE IF THERE WERE ANY TIMES WHEN I FORGOT TO GIVE HER WATER OR FOOD.

there was that **vacation** in april...

SHE CLEARS HER THROAT AND BEGINS TO SPEAK.

≷ahem≷

basically things have been pretty good.

I'M RELIEVED. AFTER THE REPORTERS DEPART, I ASK HER WHY SHE NEVER SPOKE BEFORE.

well, i've never been **interviewed** before...

From a dream by Eva Belanger

I DREAMT I WAS FIGHTING DARTH VADER TO THE DEATH!

INSTEAD OF STORM TROOPERS, THE EMPIRE WAS NOW EMPLOYING MIGRANT FARM WORKERS.

IN THE HEAT OF BATTLE, MY LIGHT SABER RAN OUT OF BATTERIES.

aww crap.

BUT I DEFEATED DARTH ANYWAY USING THE POWER OF LOVE.

it's going to be ok.

From a dream by Ray Jewel

IN P.E. CLASS WE PLAYED A GAME LIKE DODGE BALL, EXCEPT THE OTHER TEAM THREW PICKLES.

THERE WAS ALSO THIS BASKETBALL HOOP, AND IF YOU MADE A BASKET YOU GOT FIVE DOLLARS.

THE OTHER TEAM WAS REALLY STUPID AND DIDN'T THROW PICKLES NEAR THE HOOP.

SO ME AND MY FRIENDS KEPT MAKING BASKETS AND EARNING MONEY!

From a dream by Emily Clark

IN THE LIVING ROOM SAT A BULLDOG. I HELD A PILL THAT I KNEW I HAD TO FEED TO THE DOG.

WHEN I OPENED ITS MOUTH I DISCOVERED IT HAD A "ROLODEX" OF TONGUES, EACH WITH AN ALPHABET TAB ON IT.

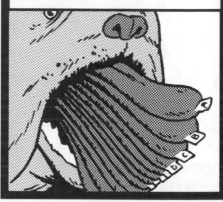

I FLIPPED THROUGH THEM BUT KEPT FORGETTING WHERE, ALPHABETICALLY, THE PILL BELONGED.

AS I BECAME MORE AND MORE FRUSTRATED, THE DOG REMAINED CALM — IT NEVER FIDGETED OR GROWLED.

was it "q"? ...no – "y"?! aargh!

From a dream by Bill Conlon

LAST NIGHT I DREAMT THAT I WENT BACK TO COLLEGE, BUT NOTHING WAS RIGHT ABOUT IT.

MOST OF MY CLASSES WERE HELD UNDERWATER. I HAD MY SCUBA GEAR BUT I WAS DISORIENTED.

CORAL HALL

PLUS THERE WERE TOO MANY FISH IN THE WATER TO PAY ATTENTION TO THE LECTURES.

IT MADE ME FEEL UNCOMFORTABLE, AND WHEN I CAME UP FOR AIR, I HIT MY MOUTH ON A ROCK.

snif snif wahh

From a dream by Lex Spahr

From a dream by Ranjit Bhatnagar

I HAD THIS DREAM THAT I WAS DATING A REALLY BIG, OAFY GUY.

I WANTED TO BREAK UP WITH HIM, BUT I WASN'T SURE HOW TO DO IT KINDLY.

SO I DECIDED TO SCARE HIM, BY PRETENDING I WAS A VAMPIRE.

these **plastic** teeth will fool him.

AS I TURNED AROUND, MY PLASTIC TEETH FELL OUT. ODDLY ENOUGH, HE HAD THE SAME IDEA — BUT HIS TEETH DIDN'T FALL OUT!

SHRIEK

SCARED HALF TO DEATH, I LEAPED OUT OF BED, JUMPED DOWN ALL FOUR FLIGHTS OF STAIRS, AND RAN INTO MY HOUSE ACROSS THE STREET.

yaaa!!

wait!

From a dream by Corinne Lucas

"Why does the eye see
a thing more clearly in
dreams than the imagi-
nation when awake?"

LEONARDO DA VINCI

I WAS FRANTICALLY RUNNING FROM SOMETHING, BUT OF COURSE MAKING NO HEADWAY.

COLD, WET STRINGS LATCHED AROUND MY ARMS AND LEGS, THEN YANKED ME DOWN.

WHEN IT STARTED SNOWING PARMESAN CHEESE, I REALIZED I WAS IN A PILE OF SPAGHETTI!

A TABLEFUL OF HUNGRY CLASSMATES LOOMED ABOVE. MY BEST FRIEND SAID, "I WANT THE MEATBALL."

From a dream by Vladimir Cole

EVERY YEAR ON SAINT ROSE'S DAY, A RELATIVE OF MINE BEGINS A 300 MILE JOURNEY.

TAKING NO COMPASS OR MAP, HE IS GUIDED BY SAINT ROSE ALONE, WHOSE INSTRUCTIONS TAKE THE MUNDANE FORM OF ROSE BUDS.

WHEN HUNGRY, HE EATS SMALL PETALS, BUT EVENTUALLY HE MUST TRAP ANIMALS FOR MEAT.

APPLE JUICE IS OFFERED TO THE CREATURES FOR A HEARTY LAST MEAL.

HAPPY APPLE

From a dream by Raven Hanna

A GROUP OF WEALTHY DIRECTORS IS MAKING A MOVIE ABOUT LIFE—ALL OF IT, AS IT HAPPENS.

OF COURSE THEY EDIT OUT CERTAIN PARTS, FOR THE "PG" RATING, AND ALSO TO KEEP THINGS INTERESTING.

ADDITIONAL SPECIAL EFFECTS AND EXPLOSIONS HELP SPICE THINGS UP.

I EAGERLY AWAIT THE OPENING SO I CAN FIND OUT WHAT MY NEIGHBORS HAVE BEEN UP TO.

From a dream by Jason Nelson

23

MY MOM AND I HIRED A PRIVATE DETECTIVE COZ WE THOUGHT SOMEONE WAS STALKING US.

stay back from the **window!**

SUDDENLY PINK FOAM SQUIRTED OUT FROM THE SHADE. IF IT TOUCHED US, IT WOULD BURN!

see, i **told** you.

THEN I PUT A RECORD ON THE BATHTUB FAUCET. IT BEGAN SPINNING, AND THROUGH IT I COULD TALK TO "THE MONKEES."

davey, will you come to my birthday party?

oh thanks! i'll **think** about it.

MICKEY AGREED TO COME, BUT MICHAEL NESMITH FLATLY REFUSED. HE WAS QUITE RUDE ABOUT IT.

uh, i'd **rather** not...

From a dream by Sarah Mitchell

THERE IS AN ESTABLISH-MENT CALLED "PIGS A-GO-GO RESTAURANT & BAR."

whee!

INSIDE I SEE ALL THIS TASTY FRIED FOOD. I'M ABOUT TO ORDER SOME, THEN I ASK WHAT IT IS.

oh, it's fried **pig claws**...

or any **other** pig parts.

whatever you desire.

uhh...no **thanks!**

NOW THE ENTERTAINMENT BEGINS, WITH A CHORUS LINE OF "PIG-GIRLIES."

this is such a **silly** dream.

From a dream by Noreen Wessling

25

I WAS REHEARSING A PLAY WITH A BUNCH OF ELITIST DRAMA PEOPLE I KNEW FROM HIGH SCHOOL.

in the garden? ... alone?!

with cream!

THEY AIMLESSLY YELLED OUT LINES, STRAYING FROM THE ACTUAL TEXT. I HAD ONLY ONE LINE.

oomph... no smell!

WE PRACTICED THIS SCENE OVER AND OVER, IMPROVISING THE ENTIRE TIME. I HAD DIFFICULTY REMEMBERING MY LINE.

you have to say it like it's french: fweee!

ok?

DURING THE SECOND ACT, MY JOB WAS TO SET PARTS OF THE THEATER ON FIRE— ADDING A PROFOUND, ARTSY QUALITY TO THE PLAY.

From a dream by Zach Archer

I WAS IN A MUSEUM IN CHINA LOOKING AT A RARE AND PRECIOUS PORCELAIN TIGER.

SUDDENLY HE BECAME REAL AND CHASED ME— I SCREAMED FOR HELP!

but he's so valuable...

we **can't** kill him!

we'll **never** get another one like **him.**

I GOT AWAY, BUT THE TIGER HUNTED ME AND ATTACKED ME UNTIL I FINALLY FOUGHT BACK.

RIP!
SHRED!
TEAR!
SMASH!
STOMP!

I STUFFED THE PIECES IN A BOX AND RETURNED HIM, WORRIED THAT I WOULD GET IN TROUBLE.

grrr

BUT THEY WERE ABLE TO REASSEMBLE THE TIGER.

From a dream by Victoria Culley

27

I WAS OUT EXPLORING THE UNIVERSE FOR THE FIRST TIME.

THIS WOMAN WHO WAS WITH ME HAD DONE IT LOTS BEFORE.

we need to find a star on the **edge** of the universe; the best planets are **always** there.

SHE WAS RIGHT—WE DIDN'T EVEN NEED SPACE SUITS. ONLY IT LOOKED LIKE THE PLACE HAD ALREADY BEEN COLONIZED!

are those **toyota** trucks?

THE SPACE ALIENS CAME OUT AND I JUST COULDN'T BELIEVE IT...

they look so **corny**!

short and **green**, just like in the movies!

From a dream by Ray Jewel

I'M IN A COFFEE HOUSE / BOOKSTORE. I FIND THAT MY TEETH ARE CERAMIC.

THEY LOOK REAL, BUT I BITE DOWN BY MISTAKE AND BREAK ONE.

oops.

SUDDENLY I REALIZE THAT EVERY GUY I'VE EVER DATED IS ALSO IN THE STORE.

I KEEP BREAKING TEETH UNTIL THE FRONT ONES ARE ALL GONE.

i womder ib dey cam be **glued**?

From a dream by Robin King

Last Belt in the World

I WAS ATTENDING THIS FANCY PARTY, BUT I DIDN'T MINGLE MUCH.

i know i'm being **followed**.

FOR YOU SEE, I HAD THE LAST BELT IN THE WORLD, AND THE INTERNATIONAL TERRORISTS WANTED IT.

get him!

THEY STARTED SHOOTING EVERYBODY WITH KNOCK-OUT DARTS. I TRIED IN VAIN TO GET AWAY...

THE NEXT THING I KNOW, I'M WAKING UP IN A DITCH SOMEWHERE (WITHOUT MY BELT OF COURSE).

they've **replaced** my hands!

I CAN'T SEE THE STITCHES OR ANYTHING, BUT I CAN TELL THEY AREN'T MINE.

From a dream by Will Barnes

I REMEMBER STANDING IN FRONT OF A COKE MACHINE. I THINK I WAS THIRSTY AND WANTED TO BUY A DRINK.

THEN I NOTICED A PAIR OF EYES STARING AT ME FROM THE BOTTLE OPENER.

I ONLY SAW HIS EYES AND NOSE—I DON'T KNOW HOW I COULD TELL IT WAS STING!

SEVERAL PEOPLE CLOSE BY WERE DISCUSSING HIS PREDICAMENT.

From a dream by Denise Vaughan

31

"I've dreamt in my life dreams that have stayed with me ever after and changed my ideas: they've gone through and through me, like wine through water, and altered the color of my mind."

EMILY BRONTË

I WAS AT SOME KIND OF SEMINAR WHERE YOU SIT AROUND AND SOMEBODY EXPLAINS WHAT'S WRONG WITH YOU, OR TRIES TO MOTIVATE YOU.

I TURNED AND LOOKED OUT THE WINDOW. AS MY EYES GOT USED TO THE NIGHT SKY, I COULD SEE THE STARS.

I STARTED TO MAKE OUT SOME CONSTELLATIONS— ONES I HAD NEVER SEEN OR HEARD OF.

oh that's daddy long-legs.

THEY WERE ALL REALLY STRANGE THINGS LIKE CAR PARTS, EYELASH CURLERS, AND KITCHEN UTENSILS.

there's my girl scout cooking badge!

From a dream by Eve Cairo

33

I DREAMT OF RIDING INSIDE A GIANT, TALKING BLUEBERRY WHICH FLOATED THROUGH THE AIR.

whee!

WE FLEW OVER THE PACIFIC, AND THE OCEAN COMPLIMENTED THE BLUEBERRY ON ITS BRILLIANT HUE.

why thank you.

APPARENTLY, ALL BLUE THINGS HAVE A GREAT RESPECT FOR EACH OTHER.

WE TOURED ASIA AND THE MIDDLE EAST, ALMOST GETTING SHOT DOWN NEAR KUWAIT.

look out!

THEN IN EUROPE, THE BLUEBERRY ROLLED DOWN THE ALPS. MY FRIEND FRENCHIE JOINED ME AND WE HAD BLUEBERRY PIE WHILE HITTING THE SLOPES.

From a dream by Anna Gonowon

I DREAMT I WAS AT A LAME HOUSE PARTY.

i think i'm going **home** now.

I DECIDED TO LEAVE, BUT MY CAR WAS GONE!

dude, i saw it drive off **that** way.

I TOOK OFF RUNNING IN THE DIRECTION MY CAR REPORTEDLY WENT.

FOUR BLOCKS LATER I FOUND IT, PARKED IN FRONT OF A DIFFERENT HOUSE HAVING A PARTY.

THIS PARTY WAS MUCH BETTER.

From a dream by Shawn Anderson

Cake-Horse

THERE WAS THIS HORSE, NOT JUST ANY HORSE, BUT A REAL TROTTING HORSE MADE OF CAKE—VANILLA CAKE WITH VANILLA ICING.

HE WAS VERY PUT OUT WITH PEOPLE TAKING A SLICE. BEGRUDGINGLY, HE LAY ON HIS SIDE AND LET ME CUT A PIECE.

SOMEONE SNATCHED IT AND LATER I FOUND MY CAKE IN THE BATHROOM SINK FILLED WITH WATER.

I RETURNED FOR MORE, BUT CAKE-HORSE JUST LAUGHED AT ME. IT WAS THEN THAT I NOTICED HE HAD BAD TEETH.

HAW-HAW!

From a dream by Colleen D. McManus

36

I WORKED AT THE WHITE HOUSE. PRESIDENT CLINTON WANTED TO GO FOR A RIDE, TO FIND A CHURCH.

there aren't many listed.

THEN, AT MY CHILDHOOD HOME, MOM ASKED WHERE WE'D BEEN. MY SISTER AND I REPLIED IN UNISON.

i have **nothing further** to say at this time.

NEXT I SAW CLINTON WAS MAKING A SANDWICH WITH MIRACLE WHIP. IT TURNED OUT HE WAS MY DAD!

I'D BEEN EXCITED TO RIDE WITH HIM EARLIER, BUT NOW I FELT HE SHOULD BE SPENDING A LOT MORE TIME WITH ME—HIS SON.

From a dream by Jim Stoicheff

Madonna's Tribute Show

I DREAM THAT I AM PER-
FORMING ON MADONNA'S
TRIBUTE SHOW WHEN SHE
IS EIGHTY YEARS OLD.

ladies and
gentlemen...
madonna!

MADONNA IS STILL
PRETTY AND TALENTED,
BUT SHE CAN'T DANCE
LIKE SHE USED TO.

oh...
thank
you!

SHE IS SO DEPRESSED
AND TRIES TO BE NICER
TO EVERYONE.

I ENCOURAGE HER WITH AN
AUTOGRAPH, AND SAY WE
MUST GET TOGETHER FOR
LUNCH SOMETIME. BUT I
NEVER ANSWER HER CALLS.

RING!
RING!

IN THIS HUGE VICTORIAN HOUSE, ALL MY FRIENDS HAVE BEEN EATEN BY THE GHOSTLY TRIO FROM THAT CASPER CARTOON.

I SEE THEM THROUGH THE KITCHEN DOOR KEYHOLE.

they're after me next— i **know** it.

they can **smell** me!

FRANTICALLY, I SEARCH FOR A WEAPON IN ONE OF THE KITCHEN DRAWERS.

looking for something?

HOT STUFF, THE LITTLE RED DEVIL, OFFERS ME FREEDOM IN EXCHANGE FOR MY SOUL.

well, i guess i have no other choice.

From a dream by Landry Q. Walker

39

I DREAMT THAT A PUNK ROCK BAND WAS PLAYING AT A POOLSIDE.

THE AUDIENCE STOOD IN THE POOL, DRINKING HUGE PAPER CUPS FULL OF BEER.

JUMPING OUT OF THE POOL, A FRIEND OF MINE RAN UP TO ME.

get your suit on so you can watch the **band**!

look, i've been **watching** everyone in the pool for a while...

...and **no one** has gotten out to use the bathroom—

only to get **more beer** at the shack.

think about it!!

From a dream by Carrie McNinch

AT A JUNIOR COLLEGE IN SOUTH CENTRAL KANSAS, AN INTRODUCTORY COURSE IS TAUGHT BY DEATH.

IT TRANSFERS TO MOST UNIVERSITIES, EXCEPT FOR A FEW LIBERAL ARTS COLLEGES WHO ARE SKEPTICAL OF DEATH'S ACADEMIC QUALIFICATIONS.

AT LEAST ONCE DURING EVERY SEMESTER, DEATH WILL BE ABSENT FROM CLASS. IN HER PLACE IS ALWAYS THE SAME MAN.

HE SPEAKS IN A STRONG SOUTHERN ACCENT AND HIGHLIGHTS THE LESSONS WITH STORIES OF HIS WACKY SHOPPING MISHAPS.

From a dream by Jason Nelson

WHILE STROLLING IN A SMALL CITY PARK, I SAW SIMON AND GARFUNKEL PLAYING, BUT THERE WAS NOBODY IN THE AUDIENCE.

WHEN I WALKED PAST, GARFUNKEL SMILED TO GET MY ATTENTION.

HIS EYES CLEARLY PLEADED THAT I STAY AND WATCH THE SHOW.

BUT I WAS GOING SOMEWHERE, AND BESIDES, I'D ALREADY HEARD THOSE SONGS.

From a dream by SteQve

YEARS AGO, I DREAMT OF A MAD SCIENTIST WHO INVENTED A FORMULA THAT MADE HAIR THICKER.

UNFORTUNATELY, IT MADE EACH HAIR THICKER.

From a dream by Mark-Jason Dominus

43

"*Reality*, n. The dream of a mad philosopher."

AMBROSE BIERCE
The Devil's Dictionary

LAST NIGHT I DREAMT THAT I JOINED A BROCCOLI GROWERS' UNION.

THEN I SPENT THE WHOLE DREAM JUST MEMORIZING THE BROCCOLI GROWERS' HANDBOOK.

From a dream by Lex Spahr

From a dream by Adam Shaw

From a dream by Angela Battershell

Lovable, Talking Pony

From a dream by Bob Siegenthaler

48

MY BROTHER AND I WERE GOING TO KATHMANDU, I SUPPOSE AT THE PROMPTINGS OF SOME SPIRITUAL MAGNET.

THE RENTED PLANE WAS OVERLOADED WITH PILGRIMS. WE HAD TO GET OUT AND LIFT THE SAGGING WINGS.

oh, we'll never make it over the **himalayas** now!

WITH LUCK I MADE IT TO THE INN AT KATHMANDU, BUT NOW MY BROTHER WAS MISSING.

SO I PLAYED CARDS AND DRANK. LATER I CRAWLED INTO A PILE OF FURS WITH A WOMAN I'D JUST MET.

From a dream by **Vlad Nemov**

49

From a dream by Denise Vaughan

I'M A YOUNG CHILD, VISITING MY GRANDMOTHER WITH MY MOM AND DAD.

SUDDENLY A MOOSE BREAKS THROUGH THE WALLS FROM OUTSIDE AND TERRORIZES US ALL.

AFTER THE MOOSE IS GONE, WE DRIVE UP TO CANADA.

why canada?

all mooses come from there.

THEN WE TRACK IT DOWN.

what'll we do if we find it?

i dunno. get its license number, perhaps?

OZ   21
ATLANTIS 66
CANADA   114

From a dream by Aaron Morrison

51

I'M AT A PARTY, CHATTING UP THIS GREAT GIRL.

I'M EXTREMELY ATTRACTED TO HER AND SHE INVITES ME OVER TO HER PLACE.

just one thing— i have to go ask my **wife** if it's ok.

i'd **never** cheat on her.

I'M ABOUT TO GO FIND HER WHEN I REALIZE THAT THIS GIRL I'VE BEEN TRYING TO SEDUCE ACTUALLY IS MY WIFE.

but i'm right here!

From a dream by Jim Robinson

I WAS TRANSPORTED TO A HUGE BAZAAR/MALL IN ANOTHER DIMENSION.

AT THE FAR END OF A LONG CORRIDOR, I SAW SOME PEOPLE MY AGE.

hi. i live in a city called **milwaukee,** in wisconsin ... on planet earth.

you know— the **milky way**?

THEY DIDN'T KNOW WHAT I WAS TALKING ABOUT, BUT WE EXCHANGED NUMBERS ANYWAY, TO KEEP IN TOUCH.

mwaal-kay?

?

ON THE WAY BACK I FOUND A WALLET, FULL OF EXOTIC MONEY AND CREDIT CARDS.

all right!

BUT IT WASN'T EARTH MONEY, SO I TURNED IT IN.

From a dream by Maria Rhodes

I WAS DOING A COMMERCIAL FOR SOME BREAKFAST CEREAL WITH KITTY CARLISLE, THAT ACTRESS FROM THE 30'S.

THERE WERE NO LINES— JUST A VOICE-OVER ABOUT THE PRODUCT.

CRUNCHY CRUMBS

WHILE THE ANNOUNCER WAS TALKING, KITTY TURNED TO ME.

you have a really bad haircut.

IT HURT MY FEELINGS, BUT I JUST KEPT COOL AND TRIED TO LOOK LIKE I WAS THINKING ABOUT CEREAL.

From a dream by Russ Ediger

54

I WAS IN AN OLD PACKARD CAR WITH WALT DISNEY, MAKING SMALL TALK.

everyone says that my grandpa **looked** just like you, but i never **met** him

JUST THEN A WET BLOND GIRL OPENED THE BACK-SEAT DOOR AND CLIMBED INSIDE WITH WALT.

SHE WAS HIS MAKE-OUT DATE. SUDDENLY WE WERE ALL AT A DRIVE-IN MOVIE, A REMAKE OF CINDERELLA.

WALT PROMISED TO MAKE HER A STAR. HIS HANDS DANCED ACROSS HER SHOULDERS LIKE LITTLE BIRDS, BUT IT WAS JUST A CON TO FEEL HER UP.

tweet tweet!

From a dream by Andrea Rogers

"If a little dreaming is dangerous, the cure for it is not to dream less but to dream more, to dream all the time."

MARCEL PROUST

FOR NO PARTICULAR REASON I WAS GETTING BEATEN UP BY A MOB OF HOLLYWOOD STARS.

WHILE BEING PUMMELED, I COLLECTED THEIR AUTO-GRAPHS. I MEAN, HOW OFTEN DO YOU GET TO BE WITH SO MANY STARS?

AFTER THEY LEFT, I SOLD OFF THE SIGNATURES TO COLLECTORS FOR MONEY.

THEN I COMMISSIONED A SCULPTOR TO BUILD A COMMEMORATIVE STATUE OF THE EVENT—IN WHICH I WAS SMILING!

From a dream by Pierre Dalcourt

A Very Small Hammer

MY FATHER NEEDS A VERY SMALL HAMMER TO NAIL IN A VERY SMALL NAIL.

WITH EFFORT, HE OPENS THE HEAVY DOOR TO THE HARDWARE STORE.

uurgh!

INSIDE ARE TWO SALES-PEOPLE: ONE MADE OF TIN AND ANOTHER OF EGGS.

i-i'm **sorry**, sir. we don't **have** any.

why you...

ENRAGED, HE CRACKS THE EGG MAN INTO A SINK.

THEN HE STORMS OUT, KNOWING I CAN NEVER OPEN THAT DOOR BY MYSELF AND RUN AWAY.

I DREAMT THAT A FRIEND OF MINE WAS TAKING ME TO SOME KIND OF ALL-MALE REVUE.

i don't know about this...

oh come on, it'll be **fun**!

WE DROVE TO AN OLD FARM-HOUSE IN RURAL MAINE. THE SHOW CONSISTED OF THREE DOORS, EACH WITH A TINY PEEPHOLE.

down that hallway.

I FEARED I MIGHT RECOGNIZE SOME OF THE MEN, BUT I LOOKED ANYWAY.

HAHAHAHAH

oh!

AT THE FIRST DOOR, THE MAN HELD HIS EYE TO THE PEEPHOLE AND LAUGHED DERISIVELY AT US!

BEHIND THE SECOND DOOR SAT SOME SKINNY GUY DRINKING COFFEE.

I DIDN'T EVEN BOTHER WITH THE THIRD DOOR.

From a dream by Jaki Erdoes

59

I AM AT NIAGARA FALLS, COMPLETELY SURROUNDED BY DONUTS.

I WAS ENTERED INTO SOME DONUT EATING CONTEST AGAINST CELEBRITY DOGS.

THE DOG FROM "FRASIER" WON BEFORE I HAD EVEN FINISHED TWO.

THAT DOG WAS GOOD. A LITTLE TOO GOOD.

From a dream by Paul J. Lurie

I FORWARD SOME E-MAIL, ONLY TO HAVE IT COME BACK AND ATTACK ME!

WE TRY TO HIDE FROM IT.

WE TRY SENDING IT AGAIN.

I TELL THE OTHERS TO HIDE AND FURIOUSLY WORK TO SEND IT AWAY.

From a dream by Nan Koch

61

Hummingbird Hands

SHE HAS BEEN INJECTED WITH THE MIND-CONTROL POISON.

AND UNLESS SHE CAN CONTROL HER ARMS, THEY ARE FORCED TO STRANGLE HER LOVED ONES.

HER HANDS VIBRATE LIKE HUMMINGBIRD WINGS.

PICKING UP A BANJO, SHE FORMS A BLUEGRASS BAND.

WHEN THEY BECOME FAMOUS ALL IS WELL.

From a dream by Ranjit Bhatnagar

62

From a dream by Nick Munford

ONE NIGHT I DECIDE TO RUN AWAY FROM HOME.

I GET TO A CLIFF OVER-LOOKING A LAKE. THEN A CAR DRIVES BY AND I FALL INTO THE LAKE, 100 FEET DOWN.

A CATFISH SWIMS UP AND DRAGS ME TO A PHONE BOOTH UNDERWATER.

I BORROW A QUARTER AND HE SWIMS AWAY.

hi... it's me. ...i'm at the **bottom** of the lake.

THEN I CALL MY MOM TO TELL HER WHERE I AM.

Mathematical Love Fax

I DREAMT THAT I GOT A LONG FAX FROM MANDY.

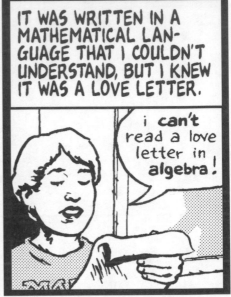

IT WAS WRITTEN IN A MATHEMATICAL LANGUAGE THAT I COULDN'T UNDERSTAND, BUT I KNEW IT WAS A LOVE LETTER.

i **can't** read a love letter in **algebra**!

I ALMOST UNDERSTOOD.... IT WAS BRILLIANT, AND I HOPED SOMEBODY COULD EXPLAIN IT TO ME.

how **thoughtful** of mandy...

FURTHER PAGES SEEMED TO HAVE ARCHITECTURAL PLANS ON THEM.

From a dream by Uncle Aussie

I WAS WATCHING TV WITH JUST ABOUT EVERYBODY I KNEW, ALL CRAMMED INTO MY LIVING ROOM.

WE DECIDED TO ORDER A PIZZA. THE PERSON WHO TOOK THE ORDER TALKED IN A SILLY VOICE.

doo yoo want **theek** crust orrr **theen**?

THE PIZZA GUY ARRIVED, DRESSED IN THIS BROWN PARAMILITARY UNIFORM.

uhh... how much?

sir! ten-twenty-three, **sir**!

WHEN WE OPENED THE BOX, OUR PIZZA HAD BUTTONS AND MARBLES AND STUFF ON IT!

...i thought you ordered **cheese and olive**?

65

From a dream by Terri Brosius

THE ALIENS WERE IN DISGUISE. YOU COULDN'T TELL THEM FROM A REGULAR PERSON EXCEPT FOR ONE DISTINGUISHABLE TRAIT.

ALIEN DIET CONSISTED OF BEER, AND NOTHING ELSE.

I KINDA SUSPECTED MY FRIEND WAS ONE, BUT SHE DISAPPEARED BEFORE I COULD QUESTION HER.

AT A RESTAURANT WITH A GIRL ABOUT MY AGE, DINNER WAS GOING SMOOTHLY UNTIL ONE OF THE WAITERS SPOKE IN A VERY LOUD AND ACCUSATORY VOICE.

you think you can **fool** us?!

(YOU KNOW THAT VOICE YOU USE WHEN YOU ANNOUNCE WHO WAS THE MURDERER IN THE GAME OF "CLUE"...?)

why don't you go ahead and order a glass of... **beer!**

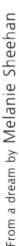

From a dream by Melanie Sheehan

"You see things; and you say 'Why?' But I dream things that never were; and I say 'Why not?'"

GEORGE BERNARD SHAW

I DREAMT I'D AGREED TO BE SHOT BEHIND MY OLD HIGH SCHOOL.

when?

we're waiting for the yard to **clear** out.

IT'S LUNCH, SO THEY'VE SLIGHTLY MISCALCULATED.

SHOOTING ME WOULD GET THIS WOMAN FROM THE STUDENT SOCIETY SOMETHING THAT SHE WANTED, SO I AGREED TO HELP.

i can't **wait** any longer!

BUT I'M SCARED. I ONLY DID THIS THINKING THAT I COULD GET AWAY.

...and i don't really want to be **shot** anyway.

Shoot me

you signed a **contract!**

aarrggh!

I TEAR IT UP, BUT THEN APOLOGETICALLY SAY I'LL TRY TO HELP HER IN SOME OTHER WAY.

From a dream by Julian Gunn

Broken Brother

I DREAMT MY BROTHER AND I WERE AT THE TABLE, AND HE COMPLAINED ABOUT A HEADACHE.

you want want me to **fix** it?

sure, thanks!

SO I GOT OUT MY TOOLS AND TOOK HIS HEAD APART, HOPING TO FIND THE PROBLEM.

hmm...

IT WAS MECHANICAL, AND I BECAME LOST IN ALL THE LITTLE GEARS AND SPRINGS.

I SHOULD HAVE LOCATED HIS INSTRUCTION MANUAL BEFORE I STARTED!

i did **mean** well.

I DREAMT I HAD LOST SOMETHING VERY IMPORTANT, SO I WENT DIGGING THROUGH MY DESK FOR IT.

INSIDE THE TOP DRAWER, TWO FIELD MICE WERE SITTING UPON A SOGGY COCKTAIL NAPKIN INSCRIBED WITH THE LYRICS TO "PURPLE HAZE."

SUDDENLY THE TWO MICE LOOKED UP AT ME, LIKE I'D INTERRUPTED THEIR CONVERSATION.

oh, excuse me.

EMBARRASSED, I SHUT THE DRAWER AND LEFT THE ROOM.

From a dream by Charla Trotman

I WORKED IN AN INDUSTRY WHICH MADE USE OF TIME TRAVEL TO FIX OR PROCURE THINGS.

ONE GUY BROUGHT IN HIS OLD VW BEETLE. IT WAS ALL RUSTED OUT, ENGINE-BLOCK CRACKED, ETC.

I SENT THE CAR, ALONG WITH A REQUEST FOR ITS REPAIR, FORWARD TO THE YEAR 3000. APPARENTLY THIS WAS WAY TOO FAR...

INSTEAD OF DOING A SIMPLE REPAIR, THEY HAD GENETICALLY RE-ENGINEERED IT TO BE A LIVING, BREATHING THING!

From a dream by Jeremy Fischer

WHEN I WAS LITTLE I HAD A DREAM THAT MY BROTHER AND SISTER AND I FOUND A BIG OPEN PIPE IN OUR BACKYARD IN WISCONSIN.

THEY WENT INTO IT LIKE ALICES IN WONDERLAND.

WE FOUND OURSELVES IN A GYMNASIUM ON THE MOON. TO AVOID DETECTION, WE TRIED MIMICKING THE MOON PEOPLE'S CALISTHENICS.

BUT WITHOUT THE PROPER ANATOMY TO PERFORM THEIR ACROBATICS, WE WERE DISCOVERED.

THEN THEY TURNED MY BROTHER INTO A FROG AND WANTED TO TEAR HIM LIMB FROM LIMB!

From a dream by Ar Thalion

I HAD A DREAM THAT MY FAMILY WAS BEING CHASED DOWN BY A GIANT AND EVIL HOT AIR BALLOON NAMED CORNELIUS.

I WAS DRIVING US AWAY AND THE CAR WENT OVER A CLIFF, BUT EVERYONE MANAGED TO JUMP OUT.

FINALLY, AFTER CROSSING THE DESERT, WE MADE IT BACK TO OUR HOUSE AND HID IN THE BEDROOM.

BUT CORNELIUS JUST SHOOK THE HOUSE AROUND UNTIL WE CAME OUT.

From a dream by Susannah Thiel

I DREAMT THAT I WAS DRIVING IN THE CITY WITH MY FAMILY WHEN IT STARTED SNOWING.

THIS SURPRISED ME BE- CAUSE I THOUGHT THAT IT NEVER SNOWED IN THE CITY.

BUT THEN THE SNOWFLAKES STARTED SPINNING AND THEY TURNED INTO BIG ICE BALL UFO'S THAT WERE SLAMMING INTO CARS, WREAKING HAVOC UPON THE CITY.

From a dream by Elizabeth Thiel

I HAD JUST TAUGHT A GOLDEN RETRIEVER TO RIDE A BICYCLE.

BUT SINCE DOGS DON'T HAVE THUMBS, HE COULDN'T STEER VERY WELL.

IN FACT HE RODE IT STRAIGHT INTO A CREEK, WHERE FRESH RAIN HAD MADE THE WATER MUDDY, HIGH AND SWIFT.

I RAN ALONG THE BANK, YELLING AT HIM.

c'mere boy! hey!

I DIDN'T CARE ABOUT THE DOG, I JUST WANTED TO GET THAT BIKE BACK.

From a dream by Ryan Budge

76

AT A LAVISH SMORGASBORD PARTY, MARY REVEALED THAT SHE HAD SECRETLY GIVEN BIRTH TO TWINS DURING THE YEAR.

i'm a **mom** — should i give her advice?

she'll need some **cereal.**

AS AN EXPERIENCED MOTHER, I HAD A LARGE CABINET FULL OF SUGARED BREAKFAST CEREALS, DOZENS OF BOXES.

I HAD BOTH KINDS OF "COCO PUFFS": REGULAR-SIZED, AND THE ONES BIG AS A BABY'S HEAD, PACKED THREE TO A BOX.

I PICKED ONE UP AND CRUNCHED A BIG BITE OUT.

they're bitterer than the tiny ones.

From a dream by L. R. Sexton

The Next President

WE WERE TRYING TO DECIDE WHO WOULD BE THE NEXT PRESIDENT.

THERE WERE MANY IMPORTANT CONTENDERS: CONNIE CHUNG, BOB DOLE, JACK NICHOLSON...

Why can't it just be me?

WE ROLLED DICE BECAUSE NO ONE COULD AGREE. WHOEVER ROLLED A TWO GOT TO BE PRESIDENT.

STRANGELY, EVERYONE ROLLED A SIX EXCEPT FOR CONNIE CHUNG.

From a dream by Ray Jewel

I WAS ON THE HUMAN SIDE IN THE COWS VS. HUMANS SOCCER GAME.

IN THE MUDDY FIELD, THE COWS HAD TAPED UP THEIR LEGS WITH ACE BANDAGES.

THEY WERE BIG AND MEAN, AND WE WERE AFRAID TO GET TOO CLOSE TO THEM.

TO COMPENSATE FOR THEIR WEAK VISION, THE BALL WAS A DAY-GLO ORANGE.

From a dream by Ranjit Bhatnagar

"**Almost every night I go back to India—a very cheap way to travel.**"

TENZIN WANGYAL RINPOCHE
The Tibetan Yogas of Dream and Sleep

From a dream by Elliott Night

From a dream by Lex Spahr

I REALIZED THAT EVERY-ONE HAS ONE "TRU LUV" AND THAT YOU KNOW IMMEDIATELY WHEN YOU SEE HIM OR HER.

WHILE I WATCHED PEOPLE PASSING ON THE BOARD-WALK, A MAN STOPPED AND LOOKED AT ME THROUGH THE WINDOW.

WE STARED, KNOWING THAT WE WERE EACH OTHERS' TRU LUV.

THEN HE WALKED ON BECAUSE THERE WAS NOTHING TO SAY.

From a dream by Pagan Kennedy

83

THE ZEN MASTER IN THE ROOM REPEATEDLY ASKS ME KOANS (RIDDLES).

tell me, what is the...

BUT EVERY RIDDLE IS ABOUT THE FILE NUMBER FOR INSURANCE FORMS.

...claim number for a 732-X96?

I ANSWER EACH WITH, "I AM THIRSTY," THEN HE ASKS ANOTHER.

THIS GOES ON ENDLESSLY.

#314-B19!

i am thirsty.

From an anonymous dreamer

AS I WAS ON MY WAY TO RIVERSIDE AMUSEMENT PARK, MY CAR BROKE DOWN. THEN I REALIZED THAT I WAS PREGNANT AND GOING INTO LABOR.

hi mom, the **car** broke down again.

IT WAS MY THIRD CHILD, NO BIG DEAL. MY MOTHER ARRIVED WITH FOUR CULT MEMBERS AND EVERYONE SAT ON THE PORCH.

I WAS DRUGGED AND LATER WOKE UP AT AN AUTOMOBILE FAIR.

but — my baby— was it a **boy** or a **girl**?

it was a hermaphrodite

I KEPT ON ASKING TO SEE HER/HIM, BUT MY MOTHER INSISTED ON WALKING AROUND THAT STUPID FAIR.

I NEVER GOT TO SEE IT.

From a dream by Sara Forrest

Psychic Cat

SOMETHING WAS AMISS AROUND OUR APARTMENT BUILDING.

IT INVOLVED THE CAT. OUR NEIGHBORS KEPT DROPPING IN WITH GIFTS, OR TO OPEN DOORS FOR HIM.

uh... he wanted out.

WE DISCOVERED THAT HE HAD GAINED MAGICAL POWERS BY AMASSING 10,000 DEAD MICE.

OUR CAT COULD CONTROL PEOPLE PSYCHICALLY!

AFTER WE FIGURED IT OUT, EVERYTHING WAS OK.

you want some gourmet cat food?

hey thanks!

From a dream by Scott Bartell

MY FAMILY AND I WERE ON VACATION, CAMPING IN THE AFRICAN SAVANNAH.

WHEN IT WAS MY TURN TO COOK, I CHOSE A RECIPE FOR CHOCOLATE LOGS.

FORTUNATELY, I HAD ALSO BAKED CHOCOLATE WOODCHIPS, WHICH WERE MUCH EASIER TO EAT.

LATER I WORRIED ABOUT DISPOSING OF THE UNEATEN LOGS SO THEY WOULDN'T ATTRACT ANIMALS TO OUR CAMPSITE.

From a dream by Janet Novak

I'M DRIVING A COMPANY CAR WHEN THIS HUGE MEATBALL COMES FLYING OUT OF THE SKY.

IT LEAVES A BIG DENT, THEN BOUNCES UP INTO THE AIR.

hey, what's the chance of **that** happening.

I SLOW IT DOWN AND—INCREDIBLY—JUST FIVE SECONDS LATER AND 50 METERS FURTHER, THE MEATBALL HITS ME ON THE SECOND BOUNCE.

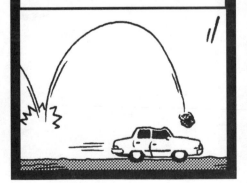

THE POLICE TURN UP AND EXAMINE THE EVIDENCE, I.E.: THE DENT AND THE MEATBALL.

lightning may never strike **twice**, but meatballs do.

From a dream by Jonathan Couper

IN MY DREAM PEOPLE ATE BATTERIES. THEY WERE IN A CATEGORY EVEN BELOW JUNK FOOD – THIS WAS "SCRAP FOOD."

SALE $1.99

YOU BOUGHT THEM IN LONG PACKAGES OF 30 OR 50 DOUBLE A'S.

THEY HAD A CRUNCHY SHELL AND A GOOEY INTERIOR.

these taste awful!

CRUNCH!

STILL, I ATE THEM 'CAUSE I WAS POOR AND WORRIED ABOUT NOT HAVING ANY ENERGY.

plus they're full of **zinc**, which is **good** for you.

From a dream by Zach Archer

Martian Architecture

I BECAME A DISEMBODIED SPIRIT AND FLOATED UP TO MARS.

I ARRIVED AT A BROAD PLAZA, OF ORNATE MARTIAN DESIGN.

IT RESEMBLED HOKUSAI'S WAVE PAINTING, CREATED BY BACTERIA CULTURES.

BUT AS I LOOKED CLOSER, I SAW THAT CORPORATE LOGOS HAD BEGUN TO NEST PERFECTLY IN THE DELICATE LITTLE SHELLS.

From a dream by John Weeks

ONE DAY I'M IN THIS ABANDONED BUILDING WHEN SOME GUY STARTS TO CHASE ME.

HIS EYEBALLS KEEP POP-PING OUT, SO HE OPENS A SUCRETS TIN, FISHES OUT A NEW ONE AND PUTS IT INTO HIS EMPTY SOCKET.

HE CORNERS ME IN THE WOMEN'S BATHROOM, THEN I SCREAM AND WAKE UP.

From a dream by Lisa Kleiber

"I don't dig nature at all. I think nature is very unnatural. I think the truly natural things are dreams, which nature can't touch with decay."

BOB DYLAN

I DREAMT THAT I WAS ON TRIAL AND SUPERMAN WAS MY DEFENSE ATTORNEY.

LAW OFFICES
Grudberg, Ladewski & Superman

I HAD BEEN SLANDERED AND HE WAS DEFENDING MY MORAL CHARACTER.

COUNTY COURTHOUSE

you've got to keep your chin up, lillian.

easy for you to say.

MY ACCUSERS SEEMED TO BE INVISIBLE OR NON-EXISTENT.

don't let them get the best of you.

THE DREAM ENDED BEFORE MY TRIAL COMMENCED.

From a dream by Lillian Hawkins

SOMETIMES I ATTEMPT TO KILL IN MY DREAMS. FOR INSTANCE, I HOLD A GUN.

I AIM AT A NON-DESCRIPT MAN WHO SEEMS QUIETLY INTERESTED IN MY ACTIONS.

BUT WHEN I PULL THE TRIGGER, ONE BULLET AFTER ANOTHER FEEBLY DROPS ONTO THE FLOOR.

POP

MY ONLY THOUGHT IS TO CONCEAL THE FIASCO FROM MY FOE, WHO IS SLOWLY GROWING ANNOYED.

whoops! ha-ha.

≥sigh≤

From a dream by Kid von Bravomail

SO I WAS LYING IN THE DESERT, TRYING TO SLEEP.

BUT THIS DOG ON TOP OF A MOUNTAIN KEPT HOWLING AT THE MOON.

awwrrrroooc

SOMEHOW I WAS ABLE TO REACH UP AND BRING HIM DOWN TO WHERE I WAS ALSO BABYSITTING TWO LIZARDS AND A GORILLA.

hey, get **down** from there!

THEN HE GOT AWAY AND RAN BACK UP THERE.

i'll **never** get to sleep.

From a dream by Sinnicam NodNarb

Gift Shop of the Damned

MY NIECE AND I WERE GOING TO A CHRISTMAS PARTY, SO WE STOPPED IN A SMALL TOWN WITH A GIFT SHOP.

let's just look in here for a **minute**

GIFTS

IT TURNED INTO A TWISTY MALL OF LITTLE SHOPS WHERE LOCAL ARTISANS MADE TINY THINGS. WE SEARCHED FOR HOURS TO FIND THE RIGHT GIFTS.

WHEN WE WENT UP TO THE CASH REGISTER, THE SALES CLERK LAUGHED.

you can't **leave!** you must stay here **forever** and make little gifts.

THEN WE KNEW—WE WERE IN THE GIFT SHOP OF THE DAMNED.

HAHAHAHA!

From a dream by Carmen Knoke

96

From a dream by Lisa Nedorost

I'M DRIVING A FREIGHT TRAIN, BUT THE FUNNY THING IS – I HAVE NO IDEA HOW TO OPERATE A LOCOMOTIVE...

96, 96... central, central mainline track 39...

...MUCH LESS UNDERSTAND THE GIBBERISH RAILROAD SLANG COMING FROM THE RADIO.

delta... to indio copy, copy...

ALL I CAN FIGURE OUT IS I AM SUPPOSED TO GET TO INDIO, CALIFORNIA. EVENTUALLY I RUN THE TRAIN OFF THE RAILS.

RAILROAD PEOPLE COME BY AND CHEW ME OUT.

nice going.

boy, you really messed this one up.

From a dream by Ron Johnson

I DREAMT THAT MY HUSBAND WAS A VAMPIRE.

HE HAD AN EVIL, PSYCHIC TREE IN THE BACK YARD THAT WOULD WARN HIM WHEN PEOPLE THOUGHT BADLY OF HIM.

ALL THIS WAS FINE, BUT WHAT REALLY DISTURBED ME WAS THE ARROGANT FRENCHMAN REDESIGNING OUR ECLECTIC COTTAGE IN A WAY I DIDN'T LIKE.

just when the **magazine** people are coming to take **pictures**!

I ESCAPED WITH MY CHILDREN THROUGH THE SECRET STAIRWAY IN THE GARAGE.

From a dream by Kelly Diels

Alien Obelisk

I AM ASSIGNED WITH SCULLY AND MULDER TO CRACK A STRANGE CASE.

A LARGE ALIEN STRUCTURE IS CONSTRUCTED RIGHT IN THE MIDDLE OF A NORTHERN TOWN. IT IS TALL, BLINKING, AND OBVIOUSLY UNFRIENDLY.

A northern town, 2:16 P.M.

THE TOWNSPEOPLE ARE WALKING BY, NOT EVEN NOTICING.

but don't you—

ah, mind your own business!

MULDER IS STARTING TO ANNOY ME. I SEND HIM ON A WILD GOOSE CHASE SO I CAN BE ALONE WITH SCULLY.

I HAD THIS DREAM WHERE I WAS AT MY GIRLFRIEND'S CHURCH. AT FIRST WE WERE SITTING APART.

AT COMMUNION EVERYONE IN THE CHURCH GOT UP, SO WE WENT AND SAT BY EACH OTHER.

I GOT UP TO GO TO THE BATHROOM AND WHEN I CAME BACK, ONE OF MY GOOD FRIENDS HAD TAKEN MY SEAT. NOW I COULDN'T SIT NEXT TO MY GAL !

THEN DURING COMMUNION WE HAD BACON, RATHER THAN BREAD AND WINE.

From a dream by Chat

Delivering Billy Joel

I HAPPENED TO BE AROUND WHEN THEY DELIVERED BILLY JOEL FOR TONIGHT'S CONCERT.

THE TRUCK PULLED UP BEHIND THE AUDITORIUM. FIRST THEY UNLOADED THE MATTRESSES, THEN THE STAR-LADEN STRETCHER.

he's sleeping.

BILLY TUMBLED OFF. (HIS QUILT HAD THE SAME PATTERN AS MINE!)

A SMALL, DROWSY CROWD FOLLOWED HIM TO THE STAGE DOOR, TREADING CAREFULLY THROUGH PILES OF SHEETS AND BEDDING.

From a dream by Ranjit Bhatnagar

From a dream by Margaret Richardson

I'M AT A RETREAT WHERE TED KENNEDY IS DUE TO SHOW UP.

I DON'T HAVE A SHIRT ON, WHICH IS PERFECTLY OK FOR THE RETREAT, BUT NOT FOR THE PRESENCE OF A PUBLIC FIGURE.

maybe i can drape my **hair** over.

THE GURU IS A GUY WHO STAYS IN A REFRIGERATOR, CURLED UP ON THE BOTTOM SHELF.

MOON MILK

I OPEN THE DOOR TO ASK IF HE'S COMFORTABLE.

sigh...

WITH MILD OTHERWORLDLY ANNOYANCE, HE SAYS YES.

"To explain the dream within a dream is a fool's dream."

ZEN MASTER DEIRYU

IN MY DREAM I WORKED FOR THE FEDERAL WITNESS PROTECTION PROGRAM.

FBI

MY PARTNER AND I HAD JUST PICKED UP A WITNESS WHO HAD TESTIFIED AGAINST A MAFIA FIGURE.

where should we **hide** this guy?

WE DECIDED TO PUT HIM AT THE BOTTOM OF AN EMPTY SWIMMING POOL.

he looks like a "tickle me elmo" doll down there.

WE GAVE HIM A LONG STRAW FOR BREATHING AND THEN FILLED THE POOL WITH MAYONNAISE.

that **tickles**.

From a dream by Bill Tjaden

I WAS ALONE ONSTAGE IN A HUGE AUDITORIUM. MANY PEOPLE WERE THERE, NONE OF WHOM I RECOGNIZED, STARING AT ME WITH HARSH, EXPECTING EYES.

AT FIRST I TRIED TO SING THEM A SONG, POURING MY HEART AND SOUL INTO IT. BUT WHEN I WAS DONE THEY CONTINUED TO STARE, WITHOUT ANY APPLAUSE.

la!

I ATTEMPTED TO DANCE, KICKING MY HEELS INTO THE AIR, DOING EVERYTHING I COULD THINK OF TO MAKE IT SPECTACULAR. AGAIN THERE WAS NO APPLAUSE!

I WAS ABOUT TO CRY WHEN A WOMAN WHO LOOKED JUST LIKE ME CAME OUT ON STAGE AND LED ME AWAY.

you can only fail **so** many times.

From a dream by Dana Hughes

I WAS WATCHING MTV, EVEN THOUGH I DON'T HAVE CABLE.

LAURIE ANDERSON GOT STUCK IN MY REMOTE CONTROL.

i'm inside.

here i am.

WHEN I TRIED TO CHANGE THE CHANNEL, SHE TURNED MY HEAD INTO AN APPLE.

I STUMBLED INTO THE KITCHEN AND FOUND A POTATO PEELER, WHICH I USED TO CARVE MYSELF A MOUTH.

please give me back my normal head.

From a dream by Larissa King

From a dream by Garvin Jabusch

I WAS CLEANING OUT THE AQUARIUM WHEN I DISCOVERED A NEW SPECIES: "SEA DOGS."

THEY WERE PASTEL PINK, BLUE, AND GREEN GREAT DANES, SMALL ENOUGH TO FIT IN MY HAND.

THEY DOG-PADDLED IN THE TANK JUST LIKE REAL DOGS, EXCEPT THEY HAD TO STAY SUBMERGED. STRANGELY THEY PANTED AND BARKED NORMALLY.

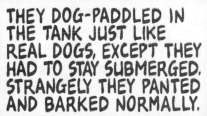

ALSO LIKE REAL DOGS, THEY WERE EAGER FOR ATTENTION SO I HAD TO STICK MY HAND IN AND PLAY "SEA BALL."

From a dream by Victoria Culley

Porn Riddance

I WAS ON VACATION IN PIGEON FORGE, TENNESSEE. MY HOTEL RESEMBLED A GIANT BARN AND FEATURED ENORMOUS PAPER MACHÉ ANIMALS OUT FRONT.

IN THE STAIRWELL I DISCOVERED THE BOX FOR A PORNOGRAPHIC FILM.

BUT PEOPLE EVERYWHERE WERE WATCHING ME. I RAN ACROSS THE STREET TO A PARK AND HURLED THE MOVIE DOWN A WATERSLIDE.

BACK AT MY HOTEL EVERYONE WAS CROWDED INTO THE LOBBY, WATCHING THE FILM. THEY APPLAUDED WHEN I WALKED IN.

I FELT VAGUELY ASHAMED.

From a dream by Marv Pratt

I DREAMT THAT HUMAN SOCIETY HAD BEEN REORGANIZED ALONG THE PRINCIPLES OF AN ANT COLONY.

EVERYONE LIVED IN A GIANT, UNDERGROUND MALL.

THERE WERE HUNDREDS OF SHOPS, THERE WERE EXTENSIVE NURSERIES FOR THE LARVAE...

wahh!

...AND THERE WAS AN AUDI DEALERSHIP.

From a dream by L. R. Sexton

What Sort of Contest?

MY GRANDMOTHER TOLD ME SHE HAD A SURPRISE; SHE HAD ENTERED ME IN A TEEN BEAUTY CONTEST!

what?!

it will be good for your **self-esteem**.

BUT IT WASN'T LOW SELF-ESTEEM THAT MADE ME THINK I WOULD LOSE—IT WAS THE FACT THAT I'M 27.

i don't **qualify**. besides, i'm not as **pretty** as a teenager.

TO MY GRANDMOTHER, THIS STATEMENT ONLY CONFIRMED HER POINT.

SO SHE DROVE ME TO THE MALL WHERE THEY WERE HOLDING THE EVENT.

THERE WE DISCOVERED IT WAS NOT A CONTEST FOR TEEN BEAUTIES, BUT FOR CHACHI LOOK-ALIKES!

i guess i have as good a chance of winning **this** one.

From a dream by Carmen Nobel

I DREAMT THAT I RODE A DADDY LONGLEGS SPIDER TO WORK.

IT WAS ONE OF THREE OR FOUR MODELS THAT SPED AWAY LIKE BUSES ON A ROUTINE SCHEDULE.

A FASTER SPIDER LEFT TWENTY MINUTES AFTER THE LUMPIER MODEL I USUALLY RODE, BUT ARRIVED AT THE SAME TIME.

ROUTINE SPIDER SCHEDULE		
MODEL	LV.	ARR.
LUMPY	7:35	
DADDY	7:55	8:02
BLACKY	8:15	8:03
CHARLOTTE	8:35	NEVER
		9:02

SO I TOOK THE FASTER ONE, NATURALLY.

From a dream by Ray Jewel

Closet Kittens

I WENT BACK TO MY OLD CHILDHOOD ROOM—IT WAS A MESS!

WHEN I OPENED UP MY CLOSET DOOR, A WOMAN CAME OUT.

SHE EXPLAINED THAT SHE HAD COME TO A PARTY AT OUR APARTMENT AND THEN GOTTEN LOST.

i ended up in your **closet**, where i had **kittens**!

AFTER THANKING ME FOR FINDING HER, SHE HANDED OVER THE KITTENS AND LEFT.

mew

From a dream by Jaki Erdoes

I WAS AN ASTRONAUT AND MEMBER OF THE CREW THAT WAS GOING TO DRIVE THE FIRST PICKUP TRUCK INTO SPACE.

THE PLAN WAS TO RACE UP A STRETCH OF HIGHWAY WITH A RAMP AT THE TOP. GIVEN ENOUGH SPEED, WE WOULD BE LAUNCHED INTO A LOW EARTH ORBIT.

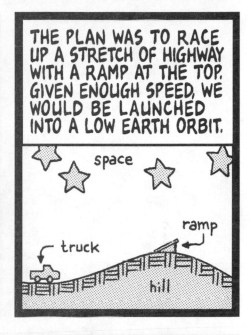

space

ramp

truck

hill

UNFORTUNATELY, ON OUR FINAL RUN, A TRAFFIC ACCIDENT WAS BEING CLEARED ON THE ROAD.

look out!

WE SWERVED AND LOST TOO MUCH VELOCITY TO REACH OUTER SPACE, MAKING IT ONLY AS FAR AS TEXAS.

From a dream by Andrew Coltrin

"If someone were to tell me I had twenty years left, and ask me how I'd like to spend them, I'd reply, 'Give me two hours a day of activity, and I'll take the other twenty-two in dreams.'"

LUIS BUÑUEL

Communal Vending Machine

I HAD JUST MOVED INTO A NEW APARTMENT WITH A CHILDHOOD FRIEND.

what's this?

there's **candy** inside!

STRANGELY, WE FIND A COMMUNAL VENDING MACHINE THERE.

WHEN SOMEONE IN THE BUILDING ORDERS CANDY, IT COMES OUT OF THE MACHINE LOCATED IN OUR LIVING ROOM.

SPONK

EVEN THOUGH IT'S LATE, PEOPLE ARE STILL DIALING IN THEIR ORDERS.

SPONK

you get this one... it's **your** turn.

BECAUSE THE MACHINE IS IN MY APARTMENT, I HAVE TO DELIVER IT. I TRY TO MAKE SMALL TALK WITH MY NEW NEIGHBORS, BUT THEY ALL ACT RUDELY.

can i just have my **change**?!

From a dream by Diana Valk

IT'S MY FUNERAL. I'M BEING LOWERED INTO THE GROUND.

THE MOURNERS TOSS CLUMPS OF DIRT ON ME.

this isn't dirt, it's cottage cheese!

I GET ANNOYED AND THROW SOME COTTAGE CHEESE BACK AT THEM.

HERE LIES DAN SCHMIDT 1968-19

SUDDENLY EVERYONE IS IN A BIG FOOD FIGHT, EXCEPT THE PASTOR, WHO DOESN'T KNOW WHAT TO DO.

From a dream by Dan Schmidt

I DREAMT THAT I WAS WORKING AT TACO JOHN'S WHEN BILL CLINTON CAME IN UNEXPECTEDLY WITH THE SECRET SERVICE.

THEY GAVE US A LIST OF SPECIAL RULES FOR PREPARING THE PRESIDENTIAL TACO, AND THE PRESSURE WAS ON!

NO OLIVES
SPICY
EXTRA
CHEESE
GUACAMOLE
PINTO BEANS

BUT I FUMBLED WITH THE SHREDDED LETTUCE, GUSHED THE GUACAMOLE GUN, AND THEN TO TOP IT OFF, BROKE THE SHELL.

IT WAS A TOUGH DAY. ON THE WAY HOME I FELL IN A RIVER. LUCKILY, JESSE JACKSON CAME OUT FROM A PARKING GARAGE AND GAVE ME A HAND UP.

MY FAITH IN LIBERALISM WAS RESTORED.

From a dream by Robert Adams

119

Relish Torture

I WON'T TALK, SO THE INTERROGATORS TAKE ME TO THEIR TORTURE CHAMBER.

INSIDE, TWO FRIENDS OF MINE ARE HOOKED UP TO THIS ELABORATE MACHINE DESIGNED FOR POPPING CONDIMENT PACKETS.

THIS IS UNFORTUNATE BECAUSE MY FRIENDS ARE A PACKET OF FANCY KETCHUP AND A PACKET OF RELISH.

aaron!

save us!!

SPLOP SPUT!!

From a dream by Aaron Jai Lee

I AWOKE IN A DIFFERENT DORM ROOM. I HAD THE SAME ROOMMATE, BUT ALL OF THE FURNISHINGS WERE UNFAMILIAR.

THE BUILDING AND FLOOR WERE DIFFERENT. HELL, EVEN THE SEASON HAD CHANGED.

PEOPLE KEPT STOPPING BY, TALKING TO ME LIKE THEY WERE MY FRIENDS.

hey, wassup?

oh— you know ...

BUT I HAD NO IDEA WHO THEY WERE, SO I JUST PLAYED ALONG, NODDED, AND GAVE NONCOMMITTAL REPLIES.

From an anonymous dreamer

Demi Moore Improves Her Act

I WAS SITTING WITH A FRIEND IN A RESTAURANT WHERE DEMI MOORE WAS DOING HER STRIPTEASE ACT ON STAGE.

WHEN SHE FINISHED, SHE JOINED US AT OUR TABLE. WE ORDERED HER SOME CHICKEN WINGS.

I TRIED TO TEACH DEMI HOW TO EAT THEM TO THE BEAT OF THE MUSIC.

you could use it in your **act**.

I REMEMBER THINKING THAT SHE WAS A FAST LEARNER.

From a dream by Veronica

122

MY BAND WAS TAKING PART IN A "WE ARE THE WORLD"-TYPE BENEFIT RECORDING, ALONG WITH A HOST OF FAMOUS DICTATORS.

ALL OF THE BIG GUYS WERE THERE—IDI AMIN, STALIN, ETC. JUST TO BE A JERK, POL POT ERASED THE ENTIRE TAPE.

I STARTED CUSSING HIM OUT, BUT WITH ONE LOOK FROM HIS EVIL EYE, I QUICKLY SHUT UP.

THE FUNNY THING IS, YEARS LATER WE ENDED UP BEING PEN PALS.

From a dream by Greg Petix

Mummy Operation

I DREAMT I WANTED TO BECOME A MUMMY, SO I WENT TO THIS DOCTOR WHO LOOKED KINDA LIKE SANTA CLAUS.

that could be **done**, sure.

I DIDN'T WANT TO BECOME A COMPLETE MUMMY—I JUST WANTED MY ORGANS REMOVED.

it'll make me look **thinner**!

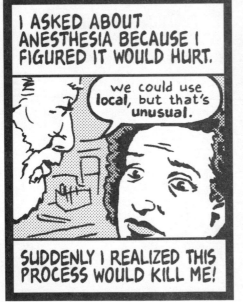

I ASKED ABOUT ANESTHESIA BECAUSE I FIGURED IT WOULD HURT.

we could use **local**, but that's **unusual**.

SUDDENLY I REALIZED THIS PROCESS WOULD KILL ME!

I STARTED TO TELL THE DOCTOR THAT I'D CHANGED MY MIND, BUT HE EXCUSED HIMSELF TO COOK PASTA.

c'mon jim—let's get **out** of here!

GLORP

From a dream by Gretchen Diehl

AT MY FRIEND KEVIN'S HOUSE, HE AND HIS GIRLFRIEND, ERICA, SHOWED ME SOMETHING COOL.

c'mon in, you gotta **see** this.

THEY WERE RAISING PORCUPINES TO SET OUT INTO THE WORLD. THE WEIRD THING WAS, THE BABIES LOOKED LIKE SNAKES.

they hafta wear **tiny** helmets, so they won't **eat** themselves.

WHILE I WAS THERE, ONE OF THE BABY PORCUPINES STARTED DRINKING FROM A LAKE OUTSIDE.

uhh... is it **supposed** to do that?

SLURP!

KEVIN AND ERICA WERE SAD BECAUSE IT DRANK TOO MUCH, AND NOW IT WOULDN'T HAVE AS MANY QUILLS WHEN FULL-GROWN.

poor little **fella**.

From a dream by Sinnicam NodNarb

Puzzle Bed

WHEN I WAS SICK LAST WEEKEND, I DREAMT THAT I COULDN'T FALL ASLEEP.

MY BED WAS ONE OF THOSE CUBE-PUZZLES, THAT I HAD TO MENTALLY ASSEMBLE.

THE ODDLY-SHAPED PIECES REFUSED TO CLICK TOGETHER.

SO I REMAINED UNCOMFORTABLY AWAKE.

From a dream by James Witowsky

Dream Resources

Dreamwork

Our Dreaming Mind by Robert Van de Castle (Ballantine Books, 1994) is a good place to begin exploring one's interest in dreams; this hefty volume contains a detailed history of dreaming and an overview of different theories about dreams, their meanings and their uses.

The Association for the Study of Dreams (www.asdreams.org) promotes "an awareness and appreciation of dreams in both professional and public arenas." It publishes the only professional journal devoted specifically to dreaming, as well as host an annual conference.

Literary Dreams

No doubt many authors have been inspired by dreams, though few have offered them up in their raw honesty. Jack Kerouac lamented that dreams were "lost at the first official recall of the pillow," but he does an amazing job of translating his in his *Book of Dreams* (City Lights, 1961).

Franz Kafka intermixes a few dreams with abandoned story fragments in his *Diaries* (Schocken Books, 1949), while William Burroughs describes many haunting dreams in his autobiography-infused *My Life: A Book of Dreams* (Viking, 1995).

Illustrated Dreams

Jim Shaw's *Dreams* (Smart Art Press, 1995) and Rick Veitch's *Rabid Eye* (King Hell, 1995) both collect snapshots of the artists' dream lives. Each night's crop gets rendered as a comic-page or montage of images. In contrast, Julie Doucet's *My Most Secret Desire* (Drawn & Quarterly, 1995) and Jim Woodring's *Book of Jim* (Fantagraphics, 1993) adapt the cartoonists' dreams (and nightmares!) into engaging comic-book adventures.

The early twentieth century saw two marvelous newspaper strips about dreams, created by the innovative Winsor McCay: *Little Nemo in Slumberland* and *Dream of the Rarebit Fiend*.

Dreaming Online

Dream Gate (www.dreamgate.com) is a terrific starting point for online dreamwork, with links to Electric Dreams (dream-sharing group and newsletter), the Dream Tree (news and events), and many other resources.

Robert Bosnak's Cyberdreamwork site (www.cyberdreamwork.com) innovatively uses the Internet for dreamworking.

New *Slow Wave* comic strips appear weekly at www.slowwave.com.

WANTED

YOUR DREAMS, a.k.a. fantasies, nightmares, ecstatic hallucinations. Last seen wearing a fake mustache and traipsing through the untended garden of your unconscious. If remembered, please send a written description to:

 Jesse Reklaw
PO Box 200206
New Haven, CT 06520

reklaw@slowwave.com
www.slowwave.com

If possible, send a photograph of yourself (it will be returned) or a physical description. Multiple dream submissions are encouraged, with no constraints on content or length. Selected dreams may be edited for clarity, brevity, or just plain whimsy.

The sleep of reason brings forth apartment chickens.